SURVIVING TRUMP

365 daily affirmations to bring peace, joy and hope back into your life

J. Lloyd

Connect with J. Lloyd at BeyondTrump@gmail.com
Follow J. Lloyd and join the conversation at twitter.com/BeyondTrump

Cover image curtesy of the most awesome and talented Ryan McGuire.
ISBN: 1540362981
ISBN 13: 9781540362988

This book is dedicated to the memory of my mother.

Up until her death in July 2016 at the age of 91, my mother was passionate about politics and was following the presidential election closely. Having come of age during World War II where she bore witness to the rise of fascism and the immense human suffering that resulted, she was terrified of what a Trump presidency could mean to the world. My mother understood all too well the often shared wisdom that those who forget history are doomed to repeat it. She never forgot. I know the results of this election would have broken her heart. So I dedicate this book to her and I promise, in her memory, to help the world once again find hope and survive Trump.

This one is for you, Mom.

Dear Reader –

People say I live in a bubble. And if by that they mean I surround myself with other people who value equality, inclusion, tolerance, diversity, environmental stewardship and respect, then yes, I proudly live in a bubble and I wouldn't trade it for anything in the world. But even in my rose-colored bubble, I never in a million years could imagine an America that could elect such a racist, misogynistic, xenophobic, divisive and unqualified person to what is arguably the most important office in the world.

To me, and millions of other proud, patriotic Americans who reject the politics of hate and oppression represented by a President Trump, it was one of the darkest days in recent history. It broke my heart. We don't know what a Trump Presidency will bring, but if we only judge it based on the hateful vision he shared during the campaign, it will be devastating for human rights, civil rights, the economy, the environment, and civil discourse.

As citizens of the world we have two choices – admit defeat and simply retreat into the darkness; or come together to heal, rebuild, organize, stay visible, and never lose sight of what is right and just in this world.

As a writer, I have always found comfort in putting pen to paper when faced with personal loss and grief. With this election, my personal loss and grief is shared with millions of other Americans, not to mention the citizens of the world who rightfully fear what this administration will mean to global order and safety. I started writing the affirmations in this book as part of my own healing process. In doing so, I realized these words might also provide hope for others; helping people stay positive and strong, and sustaining us all for the fight ahead.

The affirmations – a daily dose of positive thought and action – start on January 20th of 2017 (the day of the inauguration) and take us through the first year of Trump's presidency. While the possibility of an impeachment or resignation is extremely high - the man does have a very short attention span - if need be I will follow with a book of affirmations for year two, and year three, and year four.

This election may have pierced our bubble of safety and inclusion, but in doing so it has also opened us up to a bigger vision of what America can be and the realization that we can never be complacent and take our past civil rights victories for granted. The days ahead will not be easy, but the fight for justice and equality never has been. We are worth it. Our planet and all the living creatures are worth it. Love is worth it.

In these dark days ahead, may these daily affirmations – simple words that hold a powerful vision – bring you some peace, joy and hope. Together, we will survive Trump.

J. Lloyd, Author
November 12, 2016

Friday, January 20

I am not alone. I am one of millions of people who DID NOT vote for a government of hate and intolerance. We were the majority and our strength and resolve will move us forward.

Saturday, January 21

I am allowed to feel betrayed and angry. I am allowed to be hurt. I am allowed to be human. And when the time comes – only I will know – I am allowed to forgive.

Sunday, January 22

I am the future.

Monday, January 23

The great work begins. We have four years to reach out, connect, and rebuild. We will succeed.

Tuesday, January 24

All great movements take two steps forward, one step back, and then boom … watch out world.

Wednesday, January 25

I am a citizen of the world and my voice will never be silenced.

Thursday, January 26

I will listen to my heart always for it is filled
with love and promise.

Friday, January 27

The light is within me and it is all around me.

Saturday, January 28

Love wins. It always has and always will.

Sunday, January 29

I allow myself to cry, to feel, to release, to rebalance, to breathe.

Monday, January 30

Today my spirit soars for all that is possible.

Tuesday, January 31

I trust in myself to feel the world around me,
to touch the grace of others.

Wednesday, February 1

All around me people are organizing for change and freedom; for
each other, for ourselves.

Thursday, February 2

I am the change.

Friday, February 3

I will surround myself with people who are kind
and caring and good.

Saturday, February 4

Love rules!

Sunday, February 5

I will listen to understand. I will speak to be understood.

Monday, February 6

I hold within my heart all that is good and possible
and right in this world.

Tuesday, February 7

I honor all those who have come before me and find strength in
their courage; their sacrifice will not be in vain.

Wednesday, February 8

I hold greatness in my heart, it will never be compromised.

Thursday, February 9

The world will see me and hear me;
my voice will never be silenced.

<u>Friday, February 10</u>

The wind will blow across my face,
but I will not feel cold – I will only feel alive.

<u>Saturday, February 11</u>

My life is truly remarkable and I will
own every moment as a miracle.

<u>Sunday, February 12</u>

I believe in the inherent goodness of people and I will never let that
belief be compromised.

Monday, February 13

The world is filled with a million little miracles and I am one.

Tuesday, February 14

With love in my heart, I celebrate every day as Valentine's Day.

Wednesday, February 15

The world spins forward.

Thursday, February 16

I will never be complacent. I will never be silent.

Friday, February 17

I am surrounded by a community of people
who will never give in, who will never give up.

Saturday, February 18

The fight for justice has never been easy, but we will prevail.

Sunday, February 19

Today I will be extra kind to myself.

Monday, February 20

I will take the time to say hello to other people,
to look them in the eye, to smile.

Tuesday, February 21

Nature fills me with wonder. It wraps me with hope.

<u>Wednesday, February 22</u>

Today I will find inspiration and strength
in another person's journey.

<u>Thursday, February 23</u>

There is goodness all around me. I will let it sustain me
and fill me with hope.

<u>Friday, February 24</u>

Out of the longest nights, there still follows morning and light.

Saturday, February 25

The human spirit will always soar when faced with adversity.

Sunday, February 26

All around me I see people talking,
and organizing, and taking action.

Monday, February 27

Hope is more than a wish; it is a vision for a just and caring world
once more.

Tuesday, February 28

I refuse to give control of my life to others.

Wednesday, March 1

Together we are building a movement that will
vanquish hate once and for all.

Thursday, March 2

I hold hope in my heart; there is will blossom.

Friday, March 3

I create my own life. I own the life I create.

Saturday, March 4

The joy in my heart can never be beaten down or lost;
it is forever present.

Sunday, March 5

I am the collective energy of all who came before me,
and I hold their strength forever.

Monday, March 6

I will find wisdom from within and
I will open my mind to wisdom from others.

<u>Tuesday, March 7</u>

Loss. Grief. Healing. Strength.

<u>Wednesday, March 8</u>

The world is watching and we are not alone.

<u>Thursday, March 9</u>

The diversity of the world is a beautiful thing;
it cannot be diminished.

<u>Friday, March 10</u>

I give love to the world and I can never be diminished by hate.

<u>Saturday, March 11</u>

The truth can never stay hidden. The truth is on our side.

<u>Sunday March 12</u>

I am sorry for your anger,
but I will not let it control me any longer.

Monday, March 13

I hold the door open and encourage you to pass;
simple acts of kindness energize the world.

Tuesday, March 14

I look good today! Really good!

Wednesday, March 15

Balance comes in the totality of my life;
it is never frozen in time.

Thursday, March 16

There is new light in the world. It is all around us and
it is getting brighter by the day.

Friday, March 17

I feel the warmth of millions and millions of human souls;
we are one.

Saturday, March 18

You can never destroy a movement built on love and justice.

Sunday, March 19

When the heart and the mind work together,
everything is possible.

Monday, March 20

Hope heals.

Tuesday, March 21

I will fight for the millions of children who could not vote;
for their future, for their place in the world.

<u>Wednesday, March 22</u>

I see, I hear, I feel and I will never be silenced.

<u>Thursday, March 23</u>

We are all beautiful creatures and our love is limitless.

<u>Friday, March 24</u>

My capacity to love can never be stopped.

<u>Saturday, March 25</u>

I will learn from my anger; I will never let it control me.

<u>Sunday, March 26</u>

I am the universe; infinite and vast and one.

<u>Monday, March 27</u>

Energy pulsates through me and
it can only be channeled for good.

Tuesday, March 28

I reject words that diminish or blame others.

Wednesday, March 29

I am the reflection of peace and love in the world.

Thursday, March 30

I see hope all around me.

Friday, March 31

I will meet two new people today; just to say hello and let them know that we are all part of the same family.

Saturday, April 1

I will forgive the people who take pleasure in fooling others
and I will laugh louder than they.

Sunday, April 2

Today I will celebrate birth and all that is possible in new life.

Monday, April 3

I will find a flower and call it
the most beautiful flower in the world.

Tuesday, April 4

I will engage in the political world;
I will listen and I will remember.

Wednesday, April 5

I choose to surround myself with people
who are positive and caring and good.

Thursday, April 6

With every heartbeat, I share joy and love with the world.

Friday, April 7

I will dance freely and with abandon to the music in my heart.

Saturday, April 8

I reject labels that diminish and reduce others.

Sunday, April 9

I look in the mirror and I see beauty ... beauty ... beauty.

Monday, April 10

I will raise my hand higher than ever before,
and I will hold it there until I am seen.

Tuesday, April 11

I will reject the politics of hate and blame and
I will call you on it every time.

Wednesday, April 12

Ordinary miracles exist all around me and today
I will celebrate them all.

<u>Thursday, April 13</u>

I will look to my ancestors and I will honor their sacrifices and
I will pledge to keep their dreams alive.

<u>Friday, April 14</u>

I will allow myself to be enveloped by love …
sweet unconditional love.

<u>Saturday, April 15</u>

There is goodness in everyone and I will seek to
help those in the darkest places to find it.

Sunday, April 16

My spirit will soar today.

Monday, April 17

I will give my time to someone in need and
let them know that they are not alone.

Tuesday, April 18

I will celebrate the infinite universe and all that is possible
and all that is yet to come.

<u>Wednesday, April 19</u>

I will allow myself to feel all the raw emotions,
uncensored and unafraid.

<u>Thursday, April 20</u>

I will find peace and I will nourish it always.

<u>Friday, April 21</u>

I will dare to dream big.

Saturday, April 22

I will grieve for those I've lost and hold their memories tight. Their
love – endless and forever – will sustain me.

Sunday, April 23

There is beauty in even the darkest places
and today I will find it.

Monday, April 24

I will open my mind to a new perspective and
I will listen with compassion.

Tuesday, April 25

I will start to see new bridges everywhere I look.

Wednesday, April 26

I understand that the horizon expands forever and
there is no edge to my possibilities.

Thursday, April 27

I see beauty in your dreams and
today we will dream together.

Friday April 28

When we work together, all things are possible.

Saturday, April 29

There is always a new beginning with unlimited possibilities.

Sunday, April 30

The fire is burning within me;
it cannot be extinguished anymore.

Monday, May 1

I find strength in nature and the continuous cycle of rebirth.

Tuesday, May 2

When I open myself to love,
I see beauty and acceptance everywhere.

Wednesday, May 3

Our love will surround their hate; our truth will surround their lies;
we will reclaim our freedom.

Thursday, May 4

I will find greatness in service to others.

Friday, May 5

I will understand that others have hidden pain,
and I will be gentle as I hold their hand.

Saturday, May 6

I will expand my knowledge of what others think
and I will not judge; I will only just take it in.

Sunday, May 7

I take my place in the world and
I will never let my voice be silenced.

Monday, May 8

I may fall from time to time, but I will never stay down.

Tuesday, May 9

I have a thousand doors yet to open;
limitless opportunities await me.

Wednesday, May 10

Within me lives greatness and power and beauty.

Thursday, May 11

I embrace the messiness of change and
will let myself live freely in the moment.

Friday, May 12

I can envision a world free of prejudice and hate and injustice.
It is within my lifetime.

<u>Saturday, May 13</u>

There is pure potential within me and all around me.

<u>Sunday, May 14</u>

I am learning from others and together we are unstoppable.

<u>Monday, May 15</u>

I am finding joy and strength by surrounding
myself with others who dare to dream.

Tuesday, May 16

My life has a renewed purpose and a greater cause.

Wednesday, May 17

I embrace my future and the limitless possibilities of my life.

Thursday, May 18

Fear cannot stop me; it will only strengthen my resolve.

Friday, May 19

I admit my heart may still be broken, but it is forever whole.

Saturday, May 20

I am open to the universe and will listen freely with my heart.

Sunday, May 21

I welcome new adventures and
embrace the unknown paths still before me.

Monday, May 22

I will let me dreams run free today, unbound by any restrictions.

Tuesday, May 23

To love unconditionally is to love freely.

Wednesday, May 24

I will build bridges, not walls.

Thursday, May 25

I will find laughter and joy today and
I will celebrate the human spirit.

Friday, May 26

I am boundless energy; destined to do great things.

Saturday, May 27

It is okay to hold myself a little tighter; to forge my own shelter.

Sunday, May 28

When I receive love it stays forever in my heart.

Monday, May 29

We continue to organize and soon our collective voices will over-whelm those who hate.

Tuesday, May 30

Allow yourself to feel lost from time to time;
trust that a new path will guide you home.

Wednesday, May 31

The future is ours to own; ours to embrace.

Thursday, June 1

Find refuge in those who hold you tight.

Friday, June 2

I trust in the collective conscious of all those who were, and all those who are, and all those who will ever be.

Saturday, June 3

My capacity to love is infinite.

Sunday, June 4

I will tune out the noise and listen to my own wisdom.

Monday, June 5

I believe in myself and my capacity to create positive change.

Tuesday, June 6

All things are possible and I will never let go of my hope.

Wednesday, June 7

I will let the goodness that surrounds me inspire my heart.

Thursday, June 8

I will open my mind to the wisdom of others
and find new truths to propel myself forward.

Friday, June 9

I will not be isolated from the community.

Saturday, June 10

I am one with the universe and its infinite possibilities.

Sunday, June 11

I will take care of myself to remain healthy and strong
in the face of adversity.

Monday, June 12

A new week gives me new possibilities for greatness.

Tuesday, June 13

I accept love from others who see my goodness
and my humanity.

Wednesday, June 14

I can be alone and feel at peace with myself.

Thursday, June 15

I feel strong and ready to continue the fight for justice.

Friday, June 16

I will not be afraid to speak my truth.

Saturday, June 17

I feel energized today, ready to take on the world.

Sunday, June 18

I am full of the light of endless possibilities.

Monday, June 19

I feel confident in who I am and
all that I have to offer to others.

Tuesday, June 20

I believe that things will get better, that our time will come, that I
will once again be fully embraced as a citizen of this world.

Wednesday, June 21

I celebrate the summer solstice and surround myself with sunlight
and warmth.

Thursday, June 22

I will allow time to heal my wounds but
never to soften my resolve.

Friday, June 23

I embrace the raw and unfinished talent
that pulses through my veins.

Saturday, June 24

I will not avert my eyes to the struggles that surround me, I will embrace my brothers and sisters with love and hope.

Sunday, June 25

I will listen to every moment today; I will feel every heartbeat.

Monday, June 26

There is incredible courage within me.

Tuesday, June 27

I will trust in my instincts and listen to my heart above all else.

Wednesday June 28

I am an incredibly beautiful person, inside and out.

Thursday, June 29

I will reflect hope and love to all those whose lives I touch today.

Friday, June 30

There is great power in unity and I surround myself with a million other voices who cry out for justice.

Saturday, July 1

I will not hide my eyes from the truth; the world is watching.

Sunday, July 2

I mourn for what could have been, but I hold hope for
what will follow the darkness.

Monday, July 3

My heart burns with the fire of justice.

Tuesday, July 4

I celebrate all that America stands for and
will always keep the dream alive.

Wednesday, July 5

I am the American dream and
it will never be tarnished with hate.

Thursday, July 6

I celebrate love and peace and hope.

Friday, July 7

I know that this hurt will pass and we will rebuild;
greater and stronger than ever.

Saturday, July 8

I will be stronger; this will not defeat me.

Sunday, July 9

I believe in love over hate.

Monday, July 10

Even when the path is steep and winds out of sight,
I will keep moving forward.

Tuesday, July 11

I will resist the urge to judge others;
instead I will focus on my own actions.

Wednesday, July 12

I will escape the hate on social media and
not engage with its perpetrators.

<u>Thursday, July 13</u>

My mind is a beautiful creation and
I will nourish it with wisdom.

<u>Friday, July 14</u>

I am unlimited in my potential for greatness.

<u>Saturday, July 15</u>

I reach out to others and find strength and solidarity in connecting
with my community.

Sunday, July 16

I am amazed at how much light surrounds me
and I bask in its warmth.

Monday, July 17

I feel empowered by my own spirit and the fight for change
I see all around me.

Tuesday, July 18

I am optimistic today; I can see a better future.

Wednesday, July 19

I am thankful for all the blessings that fill my life with hope.

Thursday, July 20

Half a year into the darkness, and I am not going away;
I am stronger than ever.

Friday, July 21

I feel harmonious today; in balance with the world.

Saturday, July 22

My passion for justice will never be diminished.

Sunday, July 23

I seek to understand and to learn and to grow.

Monday, July 24

I am positive energy and I share it with the universe today.

<u>Tuesday, July 25</u>

My heart is expanded with love and
all that is possible in this world.

<u>Wednesday, July 26</u>

The power from within is unstoppable.

<u>Thursday, July 27</u>

I am joyous because I see the future clearly and it is only good.

Friday, July 28

Today I am inspired by the joy yet to come.

Saturday, July 29

I feel the miracle of nature and find peace in its beauty.

Sunday, July 30

I am renewed and full of energy for
the great work that lies ahead.

Monday, July 31

I see love in the eyes of others and it fills me with hope.

Tuesday, August 1

The world is radiant and full of limitless possibilities.

Wednesday, August 2

I don't take any freedoms for granted and I will never stop fighting for what is right and just.

Thursday, August 3

With justice on my side, I feel calm.

Friday, August 4

I feel uplifted by the new movement for justice and equality.

Saturday, August 5

I soak in love like the sun's rays and
reflect it back into the world.

Sunday, August 6

There is change in the air and it is good.

Monday, August 7

The light may dim, but it will never be extinguished.

Tuesday, August 8

I will never let others define my values.

Wednesday, August 9

I embrace redemption and hold love
for those who were misled and used.

<u>Thursday, August 10</u>

We are one day closer to reclaiming the American Dream.

<u>Friday, August 11</u>

Hope nourishes my soul and my spirits soar.

<u>Saturday, August 12</u>

I will fill my day with grace notes.

Sunday, August 13

I take encouragement in seeing people unite for change.

Monday, August 14

I seek out small gestures of kindness and celebrate goodness.

Tuesday, August 15

My heart beats furious for righteous change.

Wednesday, August 16

Love is never the wrong answer.

Thursday, August 17

I am one of millions of heroes who will change the course of history for generations to come.

Friday, August 18

I will never shame others for their beliefs, but I will hold them accountable for their actions.

<u>Saturday, August 19</u>

In seeking justice, I take my place in history.

<u>Sunday, August 20</u>

My capacity for love is infinite.

<u>Monday, August 21</u>

I am growing stronger and wiser.

Tuesday, August 22

I will not be intimidated by others who
hold on to hate and resentment.

Wednesday, August 23

I acknowledge that change is hard, but I will never give up.

Thursday, August 24

I embrace what is righteous and good.

Friday, August 25

When our children ask WHY, I will tell them HOW we changed the course of history with love.

Saturday, August 26

I seek shelter from hate and grow stronger by the day.

Sunday, August 27

People who underestimate me will be shocked by my resolve.

Monday, August 28

My actions inspire others and the
movement grows exponentially.

Tuesday, August 29

I will watch them like a hawk
and I will never let any attack go unanswered.

Wednesday, August 30

In holding the truth, I shall never be a prisoner of deceit.

Thursday, August 31

My voice is getting louder by the day.

Friday, September 1

Hell, No!

Saturday, September 2

I reject racism and embrace all my diverse brothers and sisters.

Sunday, September 3

We are the rage and the fury and there is no turning back.

Monday, September 4

The people of the world are watching and they see me;
they hear me.

Tuesday, September 5

Hate will devour itself while my love will only grow stronger.

Wednesday, September 6

I see hope everywhere I look.

Thursday, September 7

When night comes, I seek out the stars to guide me.

Friday, September 8

I will challenge my generation to stay informed and vigilant.

Saturday, September 9

I share in the pain of others and hold out my hand in solidarity.

Sunday, September 10

When the world feels cold, I will offer it warmth.

Monday, September 11

I will never stop fighting for what is right and just.

Tuesday, September 12

One day we will heal and the world will be glorious again.

Wednesday, September 13

When future generations ask where were you, I will proudly say I was on the front lines of change.

Thursday, September 14

I see rays of light coming from every direction.

Friday, September 15

Hope springs forward.

Saturday, September 16

I feel sorrow for those who were conned and will always welcome them back into the family of us.

Sunday, September 17

When there is darkness all around, I will be the light.

Monday, September 18

Today I will wrap my arms around the world.

<u>Tuesday, September 19</u>

Though I mourned when the path of my life
was forever changed, my true calling was there all along.

<u>Wednesday, September 20</u>

I am a most fabulous creature.

<u>Thursday, September 21</u>

This is the dawning of a new day filled with hope and promise.

Friday, September 22

I relish small victories and exalt in the good yet to come.

Saturday, September 23

I will never give in to the bullies.

Sunday, September 24

I welcome love into my life everywhere I go.

Monday, September 25

In this movement I see the origin of grace.

Tuesday, September 26

Silence has always equaled death
and I recognize this is never more true than now.

Wednesday, September 27

Out of the fire will come renewal and rebirth.

Thursday, September 28

When it rains, I will jump in the puddles and splash everywhere.

Friday, September 29

I am happy again.

Saturday, September 30

I embrace my place in the soul of humanity.

Sunday, October 1

I have a chip on my shoulder, and it's huge!

Monday, October 2

I am the witness to my own power and conviction.

Tuesday, October 3

I see talent and drive and passion within me and all around me.

<u>Wednesday, October 4</u>

I am driven and nothing will stop me.

<u>Thursday, October 5</u>

The human condition is vibrant and thriving and so am I.

<u>Friday, October 6</u>

I will fight for those who cannot and
I will carry their spirit forward.

Saturday, October 7

When I allow myself to wander freely, I open myself up to the most amazing discoveries.

Sunday, October 8

I will never forget.

Monday, October 9

I am powerful and my voice will be heard.

Tuesday, October 10

The future is in our young people and I will join them in building a
world of love and equality and inclusion.

Wednesday, October 11

I will always march for justice.

Thursday, October 12

I honor all those who fought the good fight in the past and pledge
to keep fighting for justice and equality.

Friday, October 13

There is wisdom to be found in defeat and from that wisdom we will learn and grow and conquer the darkness.

Saturday, October 14

I will soar to new heights in my quest for justice.

Sunday, October 15

I will never allow myself or others to be marginalized again.

Monday, October 16

I will expand my network and reach out to others who share my values and refuse to be marginalized any longer.

Tuesday, October 17

I embrace the values of love and respect.

Wednesday, October 18

I will allow myself to be angry when they work to undermine our civil rights and I will use that anger to keep fighting.

Thursday, October 19

There lies a sleeping tiger within my soul.

Friday, October 20

I feel the collective love of my sisters and brothers who
share my battle from across the world.

Saturday, October 21

There is love everywhere; it surrounds our movement.

Sunday, October 22

I will read of past battles for civil rights and I will be emboldened by
the sacrifices of those who came before.

Monday, October 23

This may be just the beginning,
but I am ready to fight for as long as it takes.

Tuesday, October 24

I am engulfed in the possibilities for change.

Wednesday, October 25

I am the face of a new movement for civil rights.

Thursday, October 26

I will rest today; safely surrounded by
people who protect and cherish me.

Friday, October 27

I find strength in our shared humanity.

Saturday, October 28

I am writing my own history.

Sunday, October 29

To be alive is exhilarating and grand.

Monday, October 30

I am witness to sweeping changes for good.

Tuesday, October 31

Today I celebrate the power of my indomitable spirit.

<u>Wednesday, November 1</u>

All things are possible when I share my gifts with others.

<u>Thursday, November 2</u>

I will send positive energy across the world.

<u>Friday, November 3</u>

I will love myself freely and unconditionally.

Saturday, November 4

I will have faith in others and trust in the
collective wisdom of our community.

Sunday, November 5

I will allow myself to rest when I grow weary
but I will never lose heart.

Monday, November 6

I hear the people sing of hope and promise.

<u>Tuesday, November 7</u>

I embrace the seasons and I will be here for the
days and years still to come.

<u>Wednesday, November 8</u>

I will be kind to others and sensitive to their needs.

<u>Thursday, November 9</u>

I will never rest until everyone is free.

Friday, November 10

I am in awe of the universe and its ever-expanding capacity for love.

Saturday, November 11

I embrace the night and will never fear the silence.

Sunday, November 12

In my heart there is unconditional love and acceptance.

<u>Monday, November 13</u>

I dream beautiful dreams.

<u>Tuesday, November 14</u>

I will leave this world with no regrets.

<u>Wednesday, November 15</u>

My heart beats through the darkness and welcomes light.

Thursday, November 16

I will turn down the noise and turn up the love.

Friday, November 17

Everywhere I look I see people coming together.

Saturday, November 18

I feel the force of passionate change all around me.

<u>Sunday, November 19</u>

I will rise from the darkness and it will be beautiful.

<u>Monday, November 20</u>

I am powerful in my convictions.

<u>Tuesday, November 21</u>

I am finding joy all around me today.

Wednesday, November 22

There is power is unity and I will never feel alone again.

Thursday, November 23

I am thankful for those I love and those who love me in return.

Friday, November 24

I know people care about me and that gives me strength.

Saturday, November 25

I will make the world a better place simply by being in it.

Sunday, November 26

Like the air, I will rise … I will rise.

Monday, November 27

Life is a gift, and I will cherish it every day.

Tuesday, November 28

I will nourish my body, my soul, my mind, my heart.

Wednesday, November 29

I will allow myself to feel my grief whenever it demands, I will give it respect and space in my heart.

Thursday, November 30

I am a survivor … always a survivor.

Friday, December 1

There is unlimited potential in me and I will never hold back.

Saturday, December 2

I am allowing myself to thrive and
making myself stronger for the fight.

Sunday, December 3

The hate of others will never hold me back,
it inspires me to take my place in the world.

Monday, December 4

I am the part of a growing movement for justice.

Tuesday, December 5

I renounce hate and I grow stronger each day.

Wednesday, December 6

My soul is blossoming and it is beautiful to see.

<u>Thursday, December 7</u>

I overflow with joy today.

<u>Friday, December 8</u>

There is the most awesome energy that circles my life and propels me forward.

<u>Saturday, December 9</u>

My mind is brilliant and filled with positive thoughts.

Sunday, December 10

I am at peace with the past and I live each moment fully.

Monday, December 11

Others cannot control me any longer; I am the guide and owner of
my own life.

Tuesday, December 12

I have clarity of purpose and I own
all that I will accomplish today.

Wednesday, December 13

My fears will no longer control me;
they will slip away into the darkness.

Thursday, December 14

I feel vibrant energy coming from within me.

Friday, December 15

I see now; the future is full of beautiful light.

Saturday, December 16

Our impending victory will free the world's soul.

Sunday, December 17

My dreams are liberated and all is possible in this world.

Monday, December 18

I visualize a world of peace and it is real ... it is real.

Tuesday, December 19

I will offer the world kindness and grace.

Wednesday, December 20

There is a sense of hope that permeates the world and
I relish it.

Thursday, December 21

I am always watching and will never be complacent again.

Friday, December 22

Today my love is endless and I will give it to the world.

Saturday, December 23

The universe celebrates all that I have been and all that I will be.

Sunday, December 24

I am at peace with the world and hopeful always.

Monday, December 25

Beautiful calm surrounds me; I am ready for peace.

Tuesday, December 26

My passion for change is outrageous.

Wednesday, December 27

I will hold on to hope always; it will never fail me.

Thursday, December 28

I am creating the future we all deserve.

Friday, December 29

When the night comes early, I allow myself to dream freely.

Saturday, December 30

My resolve grows stronger and my spirit soars
higher and higher.

Sunday, December 31

Out of the darkness came great love and hope;
I cherish that gift forever.

<u>Monday, January 1, 2018</u>

A new beginning and I bask in all that is good and possible.

<u>Tuesday, January 2</u>

I recognize my life is an incredible adventure and
I celebrate every twist and turn.

<u>Wednesday, January 3</u>

I can love and laugh freely; my life is mine to celebrate.

Thursday, January 4

I roll up my sleeves and I prepare myself for
the great work still to come.

Friday, January 5

One step at a time, we are moving forward … moving forward.

Saturday, January 6

I feel inspired by all that is good and possible in the world.

Sunday, January 7

I denounce hate always and will never allow
myself to be fooled by false promises.

Monday, January 8

The movement for equality will never be silenced; nor will I.

Tuesday, January 9

Love will heal.

Wednesday, January 10

My spirt is miraculous and beautiful.

Thursday, January 11

The sun rises and bring warmth and hope,
as it always has and always will.

Friday, January 12

I am emboldened by the outpouring of love and support that inspires our movement.

<u>Saturday, January 13</u>

I am a citizen of the world and
I will never allow hate into my heart.

<u>Sunday, January 14</u>

Into the light always.

<u>Monday, January 15</u>

I am conquering my fears and taking my place in the world.

Tuesday, January 16

I am love.

Wednesday, January 17

I am hope.

Thursday, January 18

I believe that we will reclaim our place in the world;
our fight is righteous, our resolve unstoppable.

Friday, January 19

I will live in the light, always.

My Thoughts and Reflections

ABOUT THE AUTHOR

J. Lloyd lives with his awesome family in a bubble in Northern California. He has published a ton of stuff for some very serious publishers and has spoken at conferences and meetings throughout the world. He is a passionate advocate for civil rights, children and youth, reproductive rights, LGBTQ equality, animal welfare, the environment, and the United States Constitution. He also eats granola, but that is kind of a given.

CPSIA information can be obtained
at www.ICGtesting.com
Printed in the USA
LVOW13s0224151216
517363LV00014B/849/P